Have you read Part 1?

"These children stole the crown," said Lord Kent. "Throw them in prison."

"Stop!" said Henry. "I don't think they stole my crown."

Henry spoke to the guards. "Who has
been in this room today?" he asked.
"You and Lord Kent," said a guard.

"Nobody could have taken it out of this room," said the other guard. "We search everyone."

"The children took it," said Lord Kent.

"We didn't take it," said Biff, "and
nobody else could get in from the outside."

Chip saw something on the floor. It was
a broken arrow. He asked Henry to lend
him the magnifying glass.

"Someone tied string to the window," said Chip. "I think I know how the crown was stolen."

"Someone was in this room. Then
someone outside the castle shot an arrow
through the window. It had string tied to it."

"The person in the room put the string through the crown. Then they tied the string round this bar in the window."

"The crown slid down the string. Then
the person in the room untied the string
and left. It was easy."

"I know who stole the crown," said Henry. "You, Lord Kent. You want to stop me being the king."

Suddenly, Lord Kent ran off.

"Ha!" he shouted. "You will not be king. I will! You have lost the crown."

"Catch him!" shouted Henry. "Don't let him get away."

Biff and Chip grabbed Lord Kent's
cloak and pulled him over.

"Throw him in prison!" shouted Henry.

Henry ran out of the castle.

"Come on!" he called to Biff and Chip.

"We have to get my crown back."

Suddenly, Henry stopped running. Two
men were searching for something in
the grass.

"Keep down," hissed Henry. "Don't let them see us."

"What are they looking for?" asked Biff.

One man took the crown out of a bag.
"This is bad news," he said. "The
biggest jewel in the crown is missing."

"We must find it," said the other man.
"Lord Kent will think we have stolen it."
"It must be here," said the first man.
"I hope it didn't fall in the moat."

Chip had an idea. In his pocket was a
glass bead.

"Is this the jewel?" he asked.

"No," said Henry. "The jewel is
much bigger."

"Give Biff the magnifying glass, Henry,"
said Chip, "and stay where you are."
Biff and Chip went up to the men.

Biff held the magnifying glass over
the bead.

"Are you looking for this big jewel?"
she said. "We have just found it."

Suddenly, Biff dropped the bead. The
men bent down to get it. She grabbed
the crown and Chip pushed the men into
the moat. Splash!

Biff threw the crown to Henry.

"Don't drop it!" yelled Chip. "Now run!
You can be king after all!"

"I'm glad I'm not a king," said Chip.
"You just can't trust anyone."

"But you can trust the magic key," said
Biff. "It's glowing."

"Henry was just a boy," said Chip. "I wonder if he was king for a long time?"

"Who knows?" said Biff. "I wonder if he found that missing jewel?"